KNUC

A Pl

DAVID

PLAYSETS COLLECTION

This playset is loaned for six weeks.
If a longer loan is required for a production
or for study please inform library staff
as soon as possible
TEL: (01603 774770)
Please return all copies of the playset at the same
time. The number of copies is indicated on the
front of the mastercopy
Copies must be returned in the same condition
as when borrowed. A charge will be made for
any copies damaged or lost whilst on loan to you
An overdue charge will be payable if the playset
is returned after the due date

S

N

KNUCKLE

First presented by Michael Codron on 4th March 1974, at the Comedy Theatre, London, with the following cast of characters:

Curly Delafield	Edward Fox
Jenny Wilbur	Kate Nelligan
Grace Dunning	Shelagh Fraser
Patrick Delafield	Douglas Wilmer
Max Dupree	Malcolm Storry
Barman	Leonard Kavanagh
Storeman	David Jones
Policeman	Stephen Gordon
Porter	
The Michael Lomax Trio	

The play directed by Michael Blakemore
Settings by John Napier
Music by Marc Wilkinson

PART I

PART II

The main set is the Shadow of the Moon Club. The changes from scene to scene must always be very fast indeed. For this reason it is wiser not to drop a curtain between each scene.

Time – the present

I had to admit that I lived for nights like these, moving across the city's great broken body making connections among its millions of cells. I had a crazy wish or fantasy that some day before I died, if I made all the right neural connections, the city would come all the way alive. Like the Bride of Frankenstein.

ROSS MACDONALD

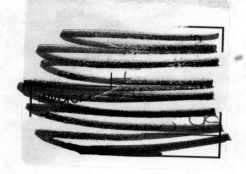

PART 1

SCENE 1

The Shadow of the Moon Club. Night.

There is a long, low bar; also a table, chairs and stools

When the CURTAIN *rises, Jenny is sitting at a table, drinking and smoking. The Barman, Tom, is behind the bar. Lomax's voice is heard on the loud-speakers.*

Lomax (*off*) Ladies and Gentlemen, dance to the music of Michael Lomax and the Freshman Three.

A hick band starts playing "String of Pearls", thin and distant

    Curly strides into the bar

Curly I'm having a lemonade.
Barman Fresh lemon, sir?
Curly Fresh lemon.

The Barman sets to. Jenny goes up to Curly

Jenny Is your name Curly?
Curly (*points to a table*) Just a moment.
Jenny Hullo.
Curly And a Scotch.

Jenny goes and sits down. The Barman holds the glass against an upside-down whisky bottle

    Bottle.
Barman Sir?
Curly I want to look at the bottle.

The Barman hands over the bottle. Curly unscrews the measuring top and takes a wet wad out of it

    Blotting paper. That's a terrible trick.
Barman Sir.
Curly If you do that again I'll squeeze the lemon in your eye.
Barman Sir.
Curly And now I'll have the bottle. (*He carries the bottle over to Jenny's table and puts it down*)

Jenny gives the Barman a nod

The Barman exits

Got you a drink.
Jenny Thank you.

Pause

You look like your sister.
Curly The Shadow of the Moon. Is this still the only club in Guildford? (*He sits at the table*)
Jenny This is it.
Curly Did Sarah come here?
Jenny You know Sarah?
Curly No, I don't. That's the whole point. I hadn't seen her for twelve years. I haven't seen anyone.
Jenny What made you come back?
Curly Was she friendly with men?
Jenny In a way. She went for a particular kind . . .
Curly I remember.
Jenny You know . . .
Curly Still the same kind?
Jenny These had a kind of Neanderthal gleam.
Curly That's them. And she was only eight at the time.
Jenny Did your father ask you to do this?
Curly Where was she working?
Jenny She'd been working as a nurse in a psychiatric hospital.
Curly Dangerous job.
Jenny Have you seen your father?
Curly Not yet. I'm staying with Patrick from tonight.
Jenny I see.
Curly How long's she been gone?
Jenny You take your conversation at a fair old lick.
Curly I'm transistorized. How long's she been gone?

Jenny insists on a pause

Jenny (*stubbing out her cigarette*) Eight weeks.
Curly Where exactly did she disappear?
Jenny Between Eastbourne and Pevensey Bay there's a stretch of beach about a mile long. Just dune and shingle. It's called the Crumbles.
Curly Had she been to Eastbourne before?
Jenny I don't know.
Curly What do the police have to say?
Jenny They think if she did drown herself in Eastbourne it would be six weeks yet before she was washed up in Herne Bay. A tribute to the strength of the English Channel.
Curly And Sarah's extraordinary buoyancy. Have a cigarette.
Jenny No, thank you.
Curly Was she suicidal?
Jenny I don't know what it means.

Curly Down in the dumps. (*He puts down the cigarettes. He never smokes himself*)

Jenny She was a paranoid. Of a particularly lethal type.

Curly Go on.

Jenny I know you don't like me, she used to say. Begging you to say, of course I like you. If you didn't say that, she was finished. And if you did say it, she didn't believe you. And once she couldn't believe that she couldn't believe anything. Everything you said had black wings and a bloodstained beak.

Curly And she was the nurse.

Jenny Yes.

Curly Have a cigarette?

Jenny No, thank you. (*She deliberately lights her own cigarette*)

Curly But not what you'd call suicidal.

Jenny She was depressed. So. Everyone's depressed. She used to say life was a plush abattoir. Fair enough.

Curly Fair enough.

Jenny She used to say—this is a very pretentious girl—she used to say she'd recognize a moment of happiness because—she remembered having one in nineteen-sixty-five, and if another came along, she could compare.

Curly When was that?

Jenny Don't know. One evening, before dusk. She felt happy. For about twenty minutes . . .

Curly Well . . .

Jenny Well—what she said—more than her fair share.

Pause. The music ends, followed by clapping

Curly Special friends, did she have?

Jenny A journalist called Dupree.

Curly Who else?

Jenny Just me.

Curly Like her pretty well?

Jenny Pretty well.

Curly Have another drink.

Jenny No.

Curly Not happy. Not liked. Pretentious.

Jenny We all told her she was pretentious. And she said certainly I am. That's because the world is unduly modest.

Curly Yes, well, there you are.

Jenny You left home much earlier she said.

Curly When I was fifteen.

Jenny She said you took four dozen rifles from the school cadet corps and sold them to the I.R.A.

Curly Old story. Not necessarily true.

Jenny Then sold the I.R.A. to the British police.

Curly That sounds more like me. I was—loud. Had the second half of the pint. That sort of thing. Smoked twenty a day. But I've quietened down.

Lomax (*off*, *over the mike*) It's Hawaiian night in the Paradise Room.

Curly gets up and helps himself to lemonade from behind the bar

(*Off*) Grass skirts, sweet music, and good food. The Paradise Room is situated on the first floor, just beyond William Tell's Alpine Grotto. Hurry up to Heaven.

A xylophonist starts playing "Under a Blanket of Blue". Jenny does not look at Curly behind her

Jenny Are you afraid?

Curly Why?

Jenny If she was dead does that frighten you?

Curly I'm not afraid.

Jenny They found a purse on the beach. And a coat. Which is how they know she was there. And inside the purse they found two railway tickets. Returns to Victoria. Which means she was with someone. Which may mean she was killed.

Curly Is that consistent?

Jenny What?

Curly Is that consistent with how she lived?

Jenny Sarah? Sure. Like all women. Hanging out for it . . .

Curly All right.

Jenny Longs to be raped. Is that not what you think?

Curly All right.

Jenny Well . . .

Pause

Curly Did she live with you?

Jenny The machine grinds on.

Curly Did she live with you?

Jenny She moved into my flat. She left Guildford to avoid her father. She ran away to Surbiton. Don't laugh. She couldn't gesture as big as you. Venezuela, wherever it was . . .

Curly Peru . . .

Jenny She ran away to Surbiton. That's the scale of her life.

Curly Had she been to Eastbourne before?

Jenny It's nice to hear the old ones again.

Curly Had she been to Eastbourne before?

Jenny Often.

Curly Why?

Jenny You could breathe in Eastbourne. That's what she said.

Curly You didn't tell me that before.

Jenny I was waiting for you to uncurl your lip.

Curly That's how I keep it. Catches crumbs. What do you do for a living?

Jenny I manage this club.

Curly Who owns it?

Jenny A man called Malloy. Runs it on the side.

Curly What else does he do?

Jenny What does everyone do in Guildford?

Curly Work in the City.

Jenny City. Right.

Curly Friend of Sarah's?

Jenny Friend of us all. This is our home.

Curly I used to come here . . .

Jenny Yes?

Curly It was skiffle. In my day. One time I . . .

Jenny Pissed in a bottle and made them sell it as Martini.

Curly You knew.

Jenny You're a legend.

Curly Sold like a bomb.

Jenny It's changed since then. It used to be the club of clubs. We all came here. Young Guildford, with our coke and benzedrine. For a lot of us it was paradise. Loud and lovely. Then it lost its way. The lushes moved in and the middle-aged voyeurs. Now it's just a bomb site. Well, you can see . . .

Curly Why do you stay?

Jenny Not your business.

Curly I'm asking.

Jenny Do you know what Sarah said about you . . . ?

Curly Nice girl.

Jenny She said whenever you stood up there were two greasy patches on the seat of your chair.

Pause. The music ends, followed by clapping

Curly I'm here for her sake. That's all.

Jenny Nobody asked you.

Curly And now I'm here I won't be put off. Nobody told me, do you know? I read it for myself, in an English paper. I reckon I'm far enough away from you all——

Jenny Don't count me . . .

Curly —to be the best person to find out what happened. I hold no brief for the Home Counties. Nor its inhabitants.

Jenny Best left to the police.

Curly They don't have my equipment. The steel-tipped boot, you know, the knuckleduster.

Jenny I can tell you've been out of the country.

Lomax (*off*) Ladies and gentlemen, for each and everyone of us there must surely come the day when—we'll gather lilacs.

The band plays a reedy introduction to "We'll Gather Lilacs"

Curly Dance?

Jenny Dance with you?

Curly It's that or go home to my father.

Jenny You're squat and ugly.

Curly I am repulsive. That is true.

(*Pause*)

Jenny Well, there you are.

Curly What I say is: don't piss in the well. One day you may want to
drink from it.

*Curly stands. Jenny begins to dance with him at arms' length. The music
swells to very loud*

Scene 2

The drawing-room of the Guildford house, Delafields. Night.

Everything is just so. As the Curtain *rises, Mrs Dunning is sitting on the
sofa, sorting clothes from a box on the floor into a suitcase on the coffee-table.
She is Scottish.*

Curly comes through the door.

Curly Good evening. We haven't met yet. My name is Curly. Patrick's son
Curly.

Mrs Dunning They let you into the country all right?

Curly No trouble. Where's Pa?

Mrs Dunning Upstairs.

Curly Have you lived here long?

Mrs Dunning About a year.

Curly fingers casually through a pile of clothes

Curly There seems very little point in storing clothes——

Mrs Dunning Yes . . .

Curly —that are well past wearing. (*He holds up an article of clothing*)

Mrs Dunning That's a gymslip.

Curly She was twenty-one. White socks and a nice school blouse.

Mrs Dunning Excuse me. (*She goes to the door*) Patrick. Somebody to
see you.

Curly Your son.

Mrs Dunning I've given you your old room. (*She sits again*)

Curly Ah, next to the boiler.

Mrs Dunning Your father is greatly looking forward to seeing you.

Pause

Patrick is a very Christian man.

Patrick swings the door open

Patrick Curly. How wonderful. How good to see you.
Curly I'm over here.
Patrick Of course you are.

Pause

Well, *Chara en thlipsat*. In the heart of sadness joy. Sit down.
Curly Thank you. (*He sits*)
Patrick Have you met Mrs Dunning?
Curly Yes, indeed.
Patrick Grace as we call her. I mean, that's her name. Grace.
Curly Sits pretty.
Patrick Good. (*He sits*)

Pause

Curly Pa . . .
Patrick Let me . . .
Curly The limits of the visit must be firmly set. You're the second on a
   list of people I'm to see.
Patrick Fine.
Curly I saw Jenny.
Patrick Nice girl.
Curly Yes.
Patrick A brightly painted object.
Curly So tell me what you know.
Patrick It was good of you to come.
Curly I was between wars. I was happy to come.
Patrick As you say.
Curly Well?
Patrick I only know what you've read in the paper. They say fifteen
   thousand Englishmen disappear every year—are never seen again.
   Amazing.
Curly But this is different.
Patrick Because she disappeared by the seashore. Not the kind of place
   where people disappear.
Curly She'd had a row with you . . .
Patrick That was a year ago.
Curly She'd left home.
Patrick A year ago. She was twenty-one. She was bound to leave.
Curly What were the reasons?
Patrick Curly, take the light bulb out of my eyes. Goodness me. Let's take
   it a little more slowly.
Curly She was suicidal.
Patrick Who says that?

Curly gets up

Curly (*to Mrs Dunning*) He can't be trusted. He drops people like eggs.
   (*He picks up a photo of Sarah as a young girl from a shelf*)
Patrick I'm not expected to run her life for her.

Mrs Dunning (*holding it up*) Exercise book.
Patrick That would have been quite wrong.
Mrs Dunning (*reading*) "Ah bonjour Monsieur le Corbeau que vous me semblez beau."

Pause

Curly Tell me the truth.
Patrick She wasn't impressed with my profession. The merchant bank. She didn't care much for yours, either.
Curly No.
Patrick But it's more glamorous than just making money.
Curly *Just* making money?
Patrick (*smiling*) I'm trying to see it from her point of view.

Pause

Curly Is that why she left?
Patrick I suppose.
Curly It wasn't more personal? (*Pause*) Had you spoken since she left?
Patrick Not really.
Curly The days I knew her she was brought up like an orchid.
Patrick Well . . .
Curly That's how she was cast.
Mrs Dunning Perhaps that was the trouble.
Curly What?
Patrick There isn't any trouble. She is highly strung. Like many of her generation without the broader based values . . .
Curly Of a traditional education. (*He replaces the photograph*)
Patrick She was unsure of herself.
Curly Did she threaten to kill herself?

Pause

Patrick She was self-critical, as you know. She thought she was a hateful kind of a person. She used to say she had contracted one of Surrey's contagious diseases—moral gumrot, internal decay. Well, that's easy to say. She could say it. But nobody else. That's the point. So here we have paranoia. The fear of other people pointing out to you what you've been saying all the time about yourself, much louder, much longer.
Mrs Dunning (*still storing*) I wonder if Alice Bands will ever come back into fashion again.
Curly And you?
Patrick What?
Curly What did you think?
Patrick I thought it was rather lame propaganda. (*Pause*) Mrs Dunning. I think we could afford a cup of tea.
Mrs Dunning Of course. (*She rises and closes the suitcase*)
Patrick Not for me.
Curly Really?
Patrick I always have mine at half past four.

Curly It's a quarter to midnight.
Patrick Another would-be decadence. Right, Mrs D?
Mrs Dunning Fine.
Curly Mrs Dunning. Use my father's old tea-bag, if you like.

Mrs Dunning goes out with the suitcase

Patrick Curly, you don't change.
Curly I recur.
Patrick Curly . . .
Curly Uh. Business, Father. Nothing at the human level, please. After all these years it would be hard to take. Just—tell me what you said to Sarah.

Pause

Patrick I've always thought that life was—volatile. You should tread light. It's not a point of view Sarah could understand. I think everyone's entitled to their own illusions. Sarah thought not. Sarah thought everyone should know everything. She told the Bishop of Guildford that his son was known as Mabel and the toast of the Earls Court Road.
Curly I see.
Patrick She said it was best he should know.
Curly What does she look like?
Patrick She's thin and angular. Wears grubby white jeans. Her hair always as if she's just been caught in a blaze. And the same expression of shock. All bones and big lips. Does that help?
Curly I . . .
Patrick How long since you saw her?
Curly Twelve years. Since I saw either of you.

Pause

Patrick I hadn't seen her for six months. She went to live with Jenny. Then one day the police came to my door.
Curly Do you think she's dead?
Patrick I do rather. It's my experience of life that it never misses a trick. And murdered as well. I expect. (*Pause*) She was like a buzz-saw in the inner ear. (*Pause*) Some man she talked to on the beach.
Curly What about the police?
Patrick That's the current theory. There's apparently a man—well-known in Eastbourne—called Dawson. Known as Dopey. Always out on the street. Reads the Bible to children. Shows them the meathook he keeps in his mac. Used to be borough surveyor. Some years ago.
Curly Is there any evidence?
Patrick Lord, no, no evidence. Sounds rather easy but it's all they've got.
Curly There's a boyfriend . . .
Patrick Dupree . . .
Curly Yeah.
Patrick Not the right type . .

Curly Not the right type for Sarah, eh?

Patrick Curly, you know better than that. Not the right type to kill. I meant.

Curly Which type is that?

Patrick Dupree is a remarkably fine young man.

Curly Solid sort of chap.

Patrick As you say.

Curly Must have been great for Sarah.

Patrick Well . . .

Curly (*breaking*) Pa . . .

Patrick The police visit me every night at eight. I will of course pass on to you everything they discover to help your—private search for justice . . .

Curly It's not justice I'm after.

Patrick I wish you well.

Curly Then tell me the truth. What about the club? The man that owns it—Malloy. Do you know him?

Patrick Of course. Stockbroker. Not very successful. His hands tremble. It's—bad for business.

Curly Is that why he bought the club?

Patrick I should think so. He's almost my age, but he seems to enjoy the company of—young people.

Curly And what does that mean?

Patrick Curly . . .

Curly Why did Sarah leave home? Tell me why she left.

Patrick (*good-humouredly*) Life with Sarah was constant self-justification. I don't propose to start all over with you.

Curly When did the Scots haddock arrive?

Patrick Grace . . .

Curly The smell of starch and clean living when you come in that door . . .

Patrick Mrs Dunning . . .

Curly I bet she dabs Dettol behind her ears.

Patrick She wasn't here then.

Curly I'd have left home if I saw that coming. I can sympathize. This place is like silver paper between your teeth. I'm back five minutes and I'm . . .

Patrick As before.

Pause

Curly (*quietly*) Don't cross your legs it spoils the crease.

Pause

Patrick Mrs Dunning is a pillar of strength. The best housekeeper I've had. You can say anything at all to her. Anything you like. Grace, you have a very large mouth and a very small heart. You could say that. She wouldn't mind. If it were true you could say that. Which it's not.

Curly Punchbag, eh?

Patrick Do you think, Curly, while you're here, a guest in my home, you could suppress the all-singing, all-dancing, all-fornicating side of your character which burst out so tellingly before you left—we do hope you've grown up.

Mrs Dunning enters with a laden tray

Mrs Dunning I did know you were coming.
Patrick Matured.
Mrs Dunning I was told to get walnut whips. Your father said you loved . . .
Curly Yes, well . . .
Mrs Dunning Walnut whips.
Patrick I wasn't saying we should have them today.
Mrs Dunning You emphasized the point.
Patrick It was twelve years ago. After all . . .
Curly Mrs Dunning . . . (*Pause*) You have a very large mouth . . .
Mrs Dunning (*with great pleasure*) And a very small heart. That's what your father always says. (*She sits and pours tea*)
Patrick I think I must be going to bed. (*He rises*)
Curly You haven't told me about Sarah.
Patrick There's plenty of time.
Curly You do want me to help?
Patrick Curly, I do indeed. Indeed I do.
Curly Then that's what I shall do. Help and then go.
Patrick Excellent. (*Pause*) We'll wait and see if you measure up.
Curly Pa . . .
Patrick Ah—we'll talk more tomorrow. Grace, my Henry James.
Mrs Dunning By the bed.
Patrick (*looking at his watch*) The light will go out at a quarter past twelve.

Patrick exits

Mrs Dunning And now we'll have a cup of tea.
Curly (*dead quiet*) Sod the tea. (*Pause*) Did you know Sarah?
Mrs Dunning I came after Sarah. I formed the impression of a tremendously vital girl.
Curly Vital?
Mrs Dunning She seemed to care so much about the world.
Curly Sarah and I went to a martello tower on Aldeburgh beach when we were youngish—I think I was thirteen—there was a poodle playing inside which followed us to the top. Sarah—me—we didn't have a great deal in common, but at that moment, together, we simultaneously conceived the idea of throwing the poodle over the side of the tower. I can't tell you why but it was a hypnotic idea. Just to see it fall. So—we lifted this grey thing up to the edge, then we released at either end, at exactly the same moment—it's the firing squad idea—you don't know who's responsible. We felt terrible.
Mrs Dunning Worse for the dog.

Curly Bad for the dog. Also. But also terrible for us. The only barbaric thing I've ever done.
Mrs Dunning You've quite a reputation as a barbarian.
Curly Ignorance.
Mrs Dunning Ah.
Curly Ignorance and jealousy. Don't tell Pa.

Pause

Mrs Dunning A wonderful man. He's undertaken an intensive study of Anglo-American literature.
Curly Micky Spillane.
Mrs Dunning He's on the *Golden Bowl*. He knows an incredible amount.
Curly For a merchant banker.
Mrs Dunning He's a cultured man.
Curly Sure he's cultured. What good does that do?
Mrs Dunning His culture enlarges his . . .
Curly Mrs Dunning. Who ran Auschwitz? A pack of bloody intellectuals.
Mrs Dunning I must go up. (*She rises*)
Curly Is he your beau?
Mrs Dunning You must have lived in his shadow. When you were a child.
Curly We thought he was a fool.
Mrs Dunning Such a tremendously clever man.
Curly The trick of making money—is only a trick.
Mrs Dunning He said he thought—you'd have grown up. (*She goes towards the door*)
Curly Do the police always call?
Mrs Dunning At eight o'clock. That's it. A typical evening. Since Sarah.

Pause

Curly What's he doing?
Mrs Dunning Reading his book. (*Pause*) Did you never like him?
Curly Not very much.
Mrs Dunning I wonder why all the words my generation believed in— words like honour and loyalty—are now just a joke.
Curly I guess it's because of some of the characters they've knocked around with. Good night. (*He picks up Sarah's photograph*)
Mrs Dunning Good night.

As Mrs Dunning turns towards the door, music—"For All We Know", with strings—fades up.

SCENE 3

Acton Warehouse. Day.

The stage is bare. A Storeman wheels on a rack of rifles, as large and as many as possible. Curly walks straight on. He takes the revolver the Storeman offers him.

The music stops.

Curly takes two steps down stage. Then he aims with great care and no fuss, and fires six times at six targets just ahead into the audience. It must look perfect

Curly We'll take two thousand Mannlicher-Carcanos, carbine and ammunition, fifteen hundred Tokarevs, fourteen hundred Mosin-Nagants, what few bolt-action Mausers you have, and the rest of the Lee-Enfields. Knock-down job lot. My client is also in the market for point thirty-o-six Springfield rifles with extra long chrome-plated bayonets. Believe it or not. And he'd also like an antique Mauser Nazi "K" series Luger for himself. As he's a bit of a raving lunatic on the side.

Curly stuffs a green wadge of money into the Storeman's pocket

And he'll be paying cash. Swiss francs.
Storeman Anything you say, Mr Delafield.
Curly And God help the poor bloody wogs.

"For All We Know" swamps the action again.

SCENE 4

The Hospital Grounds. Day.

When the CURTAIN *rises the stage is in darkness except for a spot on Curly.*

Curly Every man has his own gun. That's not a metaphor. That's a fact. There are seven hundred and fifty million guns in the world in some kind of working order. Everyone can have one like every German was going to get a Volkswagen. I don't pick the fights. I just equip them. People are going to fight anyway. They're going to kill each other with or without my help. There isn't a civilization you can name that hasn't operated at the most staggering cost in human life. It's as if we *need* so many dead—like axle grease—to make civilization work at all. Do you know how many people have died in wars this century? One hundred million. And how many of those before nineteen-forty-five? Over ninety-five million. These last twenty-five years have been among the most restrained in man's history. Half a million in Biafra maybe, two million perhaps in Vietnam. Pinpricks.

The Lights come up to reveal a stage bare except for a single bench. Max is sitting on it, slumped forward. His face cannot be seen because he is staring at the ground

Things are actually getting better. The enormous continuing proliferation of arms since nineteen-forty-five has actually led to a massive drop in the global numbers of dead. So there. I'm not ashamed of the trade, even if I'm a little tired of it. If every man on earth has a gun already, does he really need a second one? So now we can talk.

Max I asked Jenny what's his attitude to his profession, and she said—well, he says every man has his own gun, that's not a metaphor, that's a fact.

Curly It's my party piece. You sell guns, people come up to you. They can spot a moral issue. And I'm a tissue of moral issues. Like having a very loud suit. You get used to it.

Max O.K.

Curly I have to get the subject out of the way.

Max O.K. (*Pause*) Well, she worked over there. In that lovely old house. And by all accounts was a very fine nurse.

Curly What would you say was wrong with her?

Max Why does there have to be something wrong? Sarah was unhappy, that's all. She needed character massage.

Curly She wasn't ill?

Max Ill.

Curly Mentally?

Max I've written stories about this hospital for the national newspapers. One about a man who wrapped his hands in copper wire and plugged himself into the mains. Another who believes there's a colony of rats lodged in his stomach wall. He drinks Domestos. Friend. So if a girl's unhappy because her father sits smiling all day with his arse in a bucket of cream, and because she thinks her brother's a twenty-four carat shark, I don't get very worked up. As far as I'm concerned she's just ambling round the foothills of the thing, and is unlikely to come to very much harm.

Curly (*sitting beside Max*) Is that true? About why she was unhappy?

Max Certainly . . .

Curly I'd heard she was living with you.

Max (*smiling*) Neanderthal type.

Curly Well?

Max She stopped over.

Curly Lucky girl.

Max She was free.

Curly Do you think she's run away?

Max No, I don't.

Curly Do you think she's killed herself?

Max I don't understand your involvement.

Curly I'm her brother.

Max I thought she was just axle grease . . .

Curly This is different . . .

Max Make civilization work . . .

Curly You think she killed herself . . .

Max Mr Delafield . . .

Curly Mr Dupree . . . (*Pause*) One shark to another: tell me the truth.

Max I'm not a shark. (*Rising to behind the bench*) And I don't think she killed herself. (*Pause*) But, of course, she had threatened it.

Curly Go on.

Max She wasn't quite mature. She had a misleading reputation. She was known as Legover Sarah. That was fine by me. But it wasn't true. In fact she was more possessive than she appeared. She blackmailed me— (*He smiles, embarrassed*)—by saying she would kill herself. If I left her.

Curly Well . . .

Max So.

Curly Quite a man, Mr Dupree.

Max She was immature.

Curly Sure. Sure.

Max It was a terrific responsibility.

Curly Sure.

Max So when I first heard she'd disappeared I was terrified. But as soon as I heard about the purse . . .

Curly Of course.

Max Two railway tickets on the beach . . .

Curly Right.

Max I knew she couldn't have killed herself.

Curly So that's all right. (*Pause*) It's beautiful here.

Max It's a lovely place to go mad. There's a woman in there who thinks she's Napoleon.

Curly Sure. That I can understand. But who the hell did Napoleon think he was?

Max smiles

Mr Dupree, I'm told you're a Communist. What would you say?

Max Not a Communist exactly.

Curly That sort of thing.

Max Certainly.

Curly And you lived with Sarah . . .

Max Off and on . . .

Curly While entertaining other women . . .

Max That's true.

Curly Fair enough. I'm not accusing you. It seems a reasonable way of life.

Max Well?

Curly I just don't understand why a middle-aged god-loving merchant banker should describe the lazy, promiscuous, self-righteous bolshevik who's meanwhile screwing his daughter as "a remarkably fine young man".

Max No.

Curly No.

Max Perhaps Patrick just liked me. (*He moves away*)

Curly Max, what's happened to Malloy?

Max What?

Curly The owner of the club, Malloy, what's happened to him?

Max I don't know.

Curly Why would it be he doesn't answer his door? And where was he on the night Sarah disappeared? Where is he now? Where indeed were you? Do you have an alibi?

Max Of course.

Curly All good questions. Plus: how does Jenny come into this?

Max Sarah's best friend, that's all.

Curly Not bad-looking, Jenny.

Max If you say so . . .

Curly Oh, Max . . .

Max Nothing to do with me.

Curly Max. You and me. (*He gestures around him*) The real world. And Jennifer. You're not saying you've missed Jennifer. The one with the legs. And the incandescent vagina. You of all people—Max—must have noticed. Being so intelligent. And ambitious. Yet choosing to go on living in this town, when you don't have to. Letting yourself become the Guildford stringer. Tying yourself down. Why would that be? Maximillian?

Max Maxwell.

Curly Max.

Max (*sitting*) Jenny and Sarah. Of course one would see them side by side. An unfair comparison. Jenny so bright and capable and lovely. Sarah ungainly with a slight moustache. And politically—erratic, I would say, an emotional kind of conviction. Whereas Jenny soars above us all. Just—beautiful. We all grew up together, went to the same club. Sniffed the same glue. Aspirins in the Pepsi, and French kissing. But Sarah was always—loss leader. And I'm afraid it seems to fit that she was killed. No doubt by some frightfully maladjusted person. (*Pause*) And I promise you that's what I really think.

Curly I don't doubt your account.

Max Thank you.

Curly I just doubt the intense sense of relief with which you tell it. (*Pause*) I'll see you tomorrow. Same time. Same place.

Max I . . .

Curly Tomorrow.

Max goes out

(*Alone*) You chew all the meat until you hit the lump of gristle.

SCENE 5

The Delafields' drawing room. Night.

Patrick is sitting reading a sheet of music. Curly comes in.

Curly I've been to see Max Dupree.
Patrick Come in, come in. I'm reading some most enjoyable music
Curly Great.
Patrick The horns have just come in. Would you like a drink?
Curly Do you want to know what Dupree said?
Patrick I have an idea.
Curly It's all right. He's very hopeful. He hopes she was murdered. Every-one hopes that. Including you. (*Pause*) Not because you want her dead. I didn't say that. But given that she's dead you want her murdered be-cause then it's nobody's fault except some poor psychopath and there's nothing anyone can do about those. Whereas if she killed herself she's going to squat on your shoulders for the rest of your life.

Pause

Patrick Have a drink. (*He rises*)
Curly Never touch it. Time?
Patrick Ten to. The police will be here at eight. Are you staying?
Curly I'll stay—as long as I can.
Patrick You're living here . . .
Curly I know, but I couldn't last an evening. It's—what—not yet eight and already I'm half the man I am . . .
Patrick It's just lack of practice. If we tried . . .
Curly Sure . . .
Patrick Sitting together . . .
Curly Sure . . .
Patrick Having a normal conversation . . .
Curly Sure . . .
Patrick Behaving normally . . .
Curly As if I hadn't been away twelve years.
Patrick Quite so. Ten minutes to eight.
Curly O.K. (*Pause. He takes off his coat and moves to sit*) I'd be pressed—Father—to put my finger on the quality that makes you impossible to spend an evening with . . .
Patrick That subject's taboo. Anything else . . .
Curly For God's sake . . . (*He moves to leave*)
Patrick Sit down.

Curly sits

Have you read much Henry James? *Washington Square.*
Curly No.
Patrick Tremendous quality of civilization.
Curly That's what it is. (*Pause*) I'm not getting very far. The man. The

girl. And the father. She turns out to be a hysterical kind of person whom nobody likes. Least of all Max, who's meant to be the boy-friend. There's none of the innocence that word suggests. In fact an outright narcissist. And in love with Jenny I would say. Because he thought they would look good together. Walking past mirrors, that sort of thing. I don't think he enjoyed having to make do with Sarah. I should think he winced every time she opened her mouth. For myself I'd like to meet Malloy. As he must have seen Sarah every night in the club. But Malloy, everybody, has disappeared. Time?

Patrick Bit later.

Curly Yes, my friends, vanished. My day spent battering at his door. But he has gone.

Patrick What's gun-running like?

Curly (*rising*) For Christ's sake.

Patrick Sit down. I'm asking.

Curly I don't run them. I sell them. It's a perfectly legal profession. Like selling insurance.

Patrick Is there a great deal of travel?

Curly Lots. I was in Acton today.

Patrick Acton?

Curly There are one hundred and fifty thousand guns in Acton, west London. A warehouse off the A 40

Patrick I always thought you were in Peru.

Curly I go where there's a war.

Patrick Acton?

Curly Or people want one.

Patrick I thought you were in danger.

Curly There's no danger. The people who supply the arms should not be confused with the soldiers. In the trade we tend to keep soldiers at some distance. They bring bad luck. There's one man—mercenary—claims a straight flush since nineteen-thirty-nine. Indo-China, Algeria, the Congo, the Yemen, Biafra, not forgetting Hitler's war—our side, of course, Cuba, South America, back to the Congo. Then Nigeria. There's a saying in the trade.

Patrick Yes?

Curly You don't stand downwind
Of Franz Leopold von Lind.

Patrick I thought you said he was on our side in the Second World War.

Curly Eventually. (*Pause*) Pa . . .

Patrick Yes?

Curly What do you like so much about Max?

Patrick Max called me. He said he'd seen you. All you've succeeded in doing is putting his back up. I'd miscalculated. Your particular talents seem quite useless in this matter.

Curly Listen . . .

Patrick You haven't grown up. You'll never grow up until you appreciate the value of tact.

Curly I'm off.

Patrick Sit down. (*Pause*) That's typical. You've no self-control. (*Pause*) You should be happy to sit and be humiliated.

Curly moves very slightly

If you wish to destroy an ant-heap you do not use dynamite.

Curly You read them Henry James.

Patrick Just so. It's a question of noise. There is a saying in our trade. Or there ought to be. In the City. The saying is: "The exploitation of the masses should be conducted as quietly as possible."

Curly laughs slightly

Quite right. I'll tell you of an incident before she left. It made me admire—my own daughter. I don't handle money as you know. I mean, actual notes.

Curly Cabbage.

Patrick (*trying it*) Yes, cabbage.

Curly Notes are cabbage. A bank is therefore a cabbage patch and a bouncing cheque is a bruised tomato.

Patrick Good. I had the cabbage. For various reasons—to do with Grace —I came home with two-fifty in ones.

Curly You had the hots in your pocket.

Patrick Quite. I brought them back home. I'm a romantic. I put them in the piano, played "Scheherazade" and went to bed. The next morning they'd gone. And so had Sarah. She'd run away to Surbiton. (*Pause*) I was furious. It was rude and messy and—loud. But last week I went to the flat for the first time. I went into the kitchen. She'd pasted them to the wall. I admired the elegance of the gesture. It was perfectly discreet. Bless her.

Pause

Curly I saw a girl once in a bar in Laos, whose trick was an inverted sphincter. She smoked a cigarette through her arse. The most impressive feature was the hush. Just complete silence as this thing worked and blew and puffed. And nobody spoke. And the action itself was perfect. It summed up for me—the pleasures of the world.

Pause

Patrick You get the idea.

Curly Do you know what Sam said?

Patrick Sam?

Curly Sam Cummings. International arms king.

Patrick Ah.

Curly Sam said to me: "Open up. Let 'em have it."

Patrick laughs

Sam said to me: "That's what civilization was, is and will always be. Open up. Let 'em have it."

Patrick laughs again

"That is why mine is the only business that will last for ever."
Patrick Goodness me.
Curly He said that to me when I was fifteen.

Curly swings round the bottle of whisky to the table in front of him.

See that? I like the taste of whisky, Good whisky, Dad. But that's all I like. I don't like the effect. (*He empties his pockets*) Fags. Two kinds. Cigars. Sweets. Condoms. (*He puts them all down*) Do you know what I say?
Patrick No.
Curly No pleasure that isn't more pleasurable for being denied. (*He gestures at the pile*) Don't use any of them.
Patrick Goodness me.

Pause

Curly I need nothing.
Patrick Good. You're growing up.

Pause

Curly How we doing?
Patrick (*looking at his watch*) Seven minutes.
Curly Bloody good. (*Pause*) Did you ever talk to Sarah? After she left?
Patrick We met once. Neutral ground. Trafalgar Square. She took to wearing white. We had to argue things out. We talked about—no, I can't tell you . . .
Curly What?
Patrick We talked about what we believed.
Curly How disgusting.
Patrick I suppose you have to get your hands dirty sometimes.
Curly And what did she believe?
Patrick I can't remember.
Curly Well, no wonder, as you paid such close attention to her views . . .
Patrick Hush, hush over the top. Way over the top again. We don't know she's dead. And if she is, there's no purpose to be served by booting your way through the local population like a mad Hussar. This is England. Surrey. Your approach is wrong. You're peg-legging along screaming your head off fifteen paces behind the local police. You've no idea.

Curly gets up

Curly Jesus. I try to wipe my slate as clean as yours. Alcohol. Sex. I have left behind. But I still can't quite manage your state of Zen. I still have a smudge of indignation. You still drive me fucking mad. I left this house because I was sick to death with Lord Earthly-bloody Perfection. If only you'd admit . . .

Patrick What?
Curly Just—something. Just own up. For instance to your genius for mislaying your children.
Patrick Curly . . .
Curly I can't stand it.
Patrick Please.
Curly I thought when I came back you might be showing just a little petticoat below your hem. But no. (*He shows*) Perfection. (*Pause*) I'm clocking out. World champion at nine minutes. I quit the game. (*He makes to go out*)
Patrick Curly.

Curly pauses

Please take your condoms off my table.

Curly is about to exit and the music of "We Gather Lilacs" is heard, as—

the CURTAIN *falls*

SCENE 6

The Shadow of the Moon bar. Night.

Jenny is sitting at the table, crying. The Barman is behind the bar. Curly enters and goes straight to him.

Barman The lemonade, is it, sir?
Curly No. Yes. I'll stick to lemonade.
Barman Pleasure to serve you, Mr Delafield.

Curly just looks away

You know this can be a pretty wild bar some nights.
Curly Lordy.
Barman A little too wild. Without a piece.

Pause. Curly does not answer

Oh, yes. Everyone needs a piece nowadays, eh?
Curly (*half at Jenny*) Who is this creep?
Barman Right, Mr Delafield.
Curly And a Scotch, I suppose.
Barman I'm talking about a hot rod, Mr Delafield. As you call it in the trade. (*Pause*) Naturally we've got the security boys, private army, you know. But they don't have the lead . . .
Curly No . . .
Barman Perhaps you could—cross my palm with metal, Mr Delafield.
Curly Perhaps. (*He pauses, then smiles*) Open up, let 'em have it.
Barman (*smiling*) Right, Mr Delafield.

Curly walks over to Jenny with the drinks

Curly What a creep. I wouldn't sell him a water pistol. (*He sets down the bottle*) Well, Potato-face, your lucky day. This is Repulsive speaking. I am offering you a night on the tiles. What do you say? We could maybe both go look for Malloy.

Jenny You can find Malloy. Down the mortuary. (*Pause*) The wrists are cut. With the razor blade. Not easy. You really have to go at them. He went at them. So it looked like gardening shears. The only way to do it.

Pause

Curly Jen.

Jenny Who the hell am I? I bet you don't even know my second name.

Pause

Curly Have another Scotch.

Jenny What's it to you? (*Pause*) So that is why he does not answer the door. Because he is lying on the floor. With a suicide note. Bequeathing me the Shadow of the Moon. (*Pause*) Malloy had ears like a dachshund. And a voice like two trees rubbing together. In short, a slob. He liked to put a brown paper bag over his head—this will amuse you—then take all his clothes off. He did this in the company of other Englishmen of the same age and class. They ran round in circles. With straps. They never saw each others' faces. Malloy said—the pleasure was not in the whipping. Or in the paper bags. The pleasure was in going to the Stock Exchange next day and trying to work out which of your colleagues you'd whipped the night before. (*Pause*) He was funny. I liked him.

Curly Jen.

Jenny He sat in this bar, gin dripping from his chin, from his eyes, gin in the palms of his hands, talking about England. And the need to be whipped. His liver, at the end, was a little orange thing.

Curly Who found him?

Jenny I sent for the police.

Curly Does the note explain, say anything, to do with Sarah? The disappearance.

Jenny It depressed him. He says that.

Curly But . . .

Jenny But he knew nothing concrete. He'd told me that when he was alive. The note's mostly about my getting the club. He'd only bought it originally so that I could manage it. I was out of a job. So he set me up. A bauble.

Curly What did you do in return?

Jenny I did nothing. He was never my lover. It was Sarah he had. (*Pause*) Getting Sarah to sleep with you. I don't know. I imagine rather a squalid operation. Some nights you could have gathered her up off the floor, and arranged the limbs how you wanted them. She was mad about him. He spilt a whole bottle of gin all over her. She never washed for weeks. Sentimental.

Curly What . . .

Jenny (*at once*) If you shut up I'll tell you. (*Pause*) She thought he was like Patrick. Only human. She was obsessed with her father because he was so complete. Sarah used to say he had a personality like a pebble. There was no way in. Then she met Malloy. A man from her father's world. From her father's class. Of her father's age. A man like her father. But able to be agonized. Capable of guilt. She was enthralled.

Curly How long did it last?

Jenny Few weeks.

Curly Then . . .

Jenny There was a row. A few months ago.

Curly What about?

Jenny Sarah said it was about the whipping. That she'd just found out.

Curly Did you believe her?

Jenny No—the whipping would have been an added attraction. Another weakness. She'd have loved him more.

Curly Then she lied.

Jenny Sarah never lied. She said people should know everything.

Pause

Curly Have you ever met my father?

Jenny Yes.

Curly Have you seen inside the City of London? Inside the banks and the counting houses? It's perfect. Men with silver hair and suits with velvet pockets. Oiling down padded corridors. All their worries papered over with ten-pound notes and brilliantine. I first went there when I was seven. The crystal city. You could just hear the money being raked in like autumn leaves. My father moved as silkily as anyone. A clear leather desk in a book-lined room. A golden inkwell. That was all. That and the sound of money gathering like moss on the side of a west building. When he got home at night out with the cello and the Thackeray. He made his money with silent indolence. Part of a club. In theory a speculator. But whoever heard of an English speculator who actually speculated and lost? Once you were in you had it sewn up from paddock to post. Sarah would know what I'm talking about.

Jenny The two of you.

Curly So I chose guns. The noisiest profession I could find. I used to set up a client's demonstration of the AR ten. You fire tracer bullets at tin cans filled with gasoline. Did you ever see a tracer bullet hit a bean can full of petrol? It's better than a John Wayne movie. The oohs and ahs. I used to saddle up and ride into the sunset leaving the range a smoldering ruin. We sold a hell of a lot of guns. Poor Sarah. I just know what she felt.

"Blanket of Blue" is played off, Lomax-style

Let me smell your Scotch. (*He smiles into the Scotch, then sniffs*) Did anyone—love Sarah?

Jenny Bum business. Look what I got out of it. The Michael Lomax trio scraping their balls off in an upstairs room. Dipso . . .

Pause

Curly Tell me who killed her?

Jenny It would only have needed the barest suggestion. Sarah, just put your head under the water. Moving from grey to grey. She'd have done it. If you asked her. She would have covered herself in kerosene and set light to it. To win your affection (*Pause*) How Malloy could have touched her.

Curly Know what Bernie said?

Jenny Bernie?

Curly Bernie Cornfeld said to me: "Humanity's a nasty racket to be in." (*Pause*) Miss Wilbur. You see, I even know your second name. I know everything I have been able to find out. A little obscure. I know all about your great-great-grandfather, the Armenian Jew who fucked his way through the nineteenth century like an Alka-Seltzer. I know it all since you came over here at fourteen. And I know dwelling place, size of flat, name of dog, even dog's diet, even dog's distaste for Lassie meaty chunks. (*Pause*) I'm propositioning you. (*Pause*) You'd be the first for some time. For some years. The first in fact since the Sheikh of Mina Said's daughter. She went with an arms deal. A little Arab stardust might rub off.

Jenny What about Malloy?

Curly Laying Malloy aside. That's a very nice leg.

Jenny I've got another one just like it. What about Sarah?

Curly Laying Sarah aside. Listen, my dear . . .

Jenny What do you get out of it?

Curly Hopefully some change from a pound.

Jenny Listen—punk-face—I wouldn't buy what you've got if it was on refrigerated display.

Curly I don't suppose I'd be selling under those conditions. (*Pause*) You come with me.

Jenny Me Jane.

Curly I'll show you the world.

Jenny Take me to Eastbourne then. Tonight.

Curly It's late.

Jenny Don't you want to go?

Curly Go some time.

Jenny About how you were the best man for the job.

Curly All right. I'll get Pat's car.

Jenny I'll get a wrap. (*She laughs and moves to go*) Lassie meaty chunks.

Jenny exits

Curly I was once stranded in Alaska for ten days with a single copy of G. E. Moore's *Principia Ethica*. And one copy of *My Gun Is Quick*. The work of Micky Spillane. I was able in this period to make comparisons under scientific test conditions. The longest word in *Principia Ethica* is "contrahydrapallotistic". The longest word in Spillane is "balloon". Moore wins outright on length of sentence, number of words and ability to contradict yourself in the shortest space. Spillane won on one count only. It burnt quicker.

Curly exits

SCENE 7

The Delafields' drawing-room. Night.

Mrs Dunning is crocheting, Patrick reading. Peace. Patrick looks up, holds his look. Mrs Dunning looks across at him. They smile slightly. Patrick goes back to his book, sighs, puts it aside, gets up, sighs again.

Patrick Mrs Dunning.

Mrs Dunning smiles again, does not look up. He stands near her, does not touch her. She smiles at the crochet

Mrs Dunning I love it when you call me that.
Patrick Hold on.

Patrick loosens his tie, then goes out by the side door

Mrs Dunning puts her crochet aside, kicks off her shoes, then pulls off the jumper she is wearing and folds it on the sofa. She takes off her skirt, folds that, then drops a string of pearls into a little heap on the table. She stands in a bra, pants, stockings and suspenders. She gapes a moment. Pause

Mrs Dunning (*quietly*) Pat. (*She listens for an answer, then goes back to the sofa, picks up her crochet, and continues to work*)

Pause

Curly comes in from the main door, sees her, looks at his feet

Mrs Dunning sees him and half smiles. He looks at her

Patrick comes in by the side entrance, wearing only trousers and socks He stops when he sees Curly

Pause

Curly I called in on the police.
Patrick Ah.

Curly No news of Sarah. I want to borrow the car.

Patrick takes the car keys out of his pocket and throws them lightly across the room

   Curly catches the keys and goes out

Pause. Patrick stares a moment, then walks up and down. Pause

Patrick Put your clothes on. (*He moves to go out*)

Mrs Dunning turns away

Before the start of the next scene the sound of the sea is heard

SCENE 8

The Crumbles. Night

The CURTAIN *rises on a bare stage. At once, from down stage, soaking wet, Jenny comes running on, wearing a bathing costume.*

Jenny Hallelujah.

   Curly runs on, also fresh from the sea, also in a bathing costume

Curly Hallelujah.

Curly cartwheels twice. Jenny does a handstand over. Curly turns her round in a wheel, then she runs towards his out-held hands. She steps up and onto his shoulders. They stand in this position, looking out into the audience, as still as possible·

Jenny Right.
Curly So this is it.
Jenny The Crumbles.
Curly Christ.
Jenny It's strange. (*Pause*) It's cold.
Curly Cold for September.
Jenny Cold for one o'clock in the morning.
Curly What do you see?
Jenny (*with relish*) I see suffering and pain and men not happy with their lot . . .
Curly Do you?
Jenny I do. I see heavy scowls and fists raised in anger and I see tears of sorrow and of indignation. I see men with axes in their backs, acid

steaming off their skins, needles in their eyeballs, tripping on barbed wire, falling on broken bottles. That's what I see.

Curly Ah Eastbourne. Quite unchanged.

Jenny I see the living dead.

Curly What do you see that's nice?

Jenny Nice?

Curly Yeah. You know. Nice.

Jenny I see men—born happy. It just doesn't show. Let me down. (*She climbs down from Curly's shoulders*) I'm going to get dressed.

Curly Stay.

Jenny Why?

Curly Sit.

Curly sits cross-legged. Jenny watches

The colder you get the more you will enjoy being warm.

Jenny Oh yeah?

Curly The essence of pleasure is self-denial.

Curly puts a tattered paper bag on his head. Jenny just watches

I come to England maybe once a year. It's a shabby little island, delighted with itself. A few months ago I decided to return.

Jenny Where's the whip?

Curly I was ready for England. I was attracted by news of the property racket. Slapping people on top of people like layers of lasagne. Think about what I'm saying. Don't think about the cold.

Jenny Forget the cold. Listen to Curly.

Curly When I got back I found this country was a jampot for swindlers and cons and racketeers. Not just property.

Jenny goes out

(*Unaware that she has gone*) Boarding-houses and bordellos and night-clubs and crooked charter flights, private clinics, horse-hair wigs and tin-can motor cars, venereal cafés with ice-cream made from whale blubber and sausages full of sawdust.

Jenny (*off*) Forget the cold. Listen to Curly.

Curly Money can be harvested like rotten fruit. People are aching to be fleeced. But those of us who do it must learn the quality of self-control.

Jenny reappears with duffle coat and sweater. She looks warm. She is carrying Curly's clothes

Jenny Curly, is that why you came back?

Curly Wherever I've travelled wherever I've been, there's been a tiny echo in my mind. The noise in my father's office. The slight squelch of Dad's hands in the meat.

Jenny Why did you come back? (*She drops his towel near him*)

Curly takes his bag off

Curly I came back because I'm ready. I've grown up.

Pause

Jenny What about Sarah?

Curly Sarah. (*Pause*) Yes, well. That as well. (*Pause. He wraps himself in his towel*) When I went to get the car my father was with Mrs Dunning. I even detected a moment of shame. He's getting old. The first crack in the pebble. It made me sad. You should see her thighs. Like putting your hand between two slices of liver.

Jenny You horrible little man. (*Pause*) Sarah was wide-open. An ever-open wound. Her face was so—open it just begged to be kicked. You had to put the boot in. It's . . .

Curly All right . . .

Jenny She was so naïve. She used to tell Patrick your wealth is built on the suffering of the poor. And she expected an answer.

Curly All right.

Jenny (*screaming*) All right. (*She throws his clothes to the ground*) Always ready with an innocent question. Why don't you share what you've got? Why can't people run their own lives? Why persist with a system you know to be wrong? How can you bear to be rich when so many people are poor?

Curly Did she say that?

Jenny Well, what did she expect? (*Pause*) Christ Jesus. Doesn't she know there's a war on? She was asking for it.

Curly Do you know what Bernie said?

Pause

Jenny No.

Curly Bernie Cornfeld said to me: "Curly," he said, "there's nothing in this world so lovely it can't be shat on."

Jenny Right.

Curly Right.

Jenny And this is where she died. (*She yells into the night air*) Return John Bloom to your kingdom. Jack Cotton, arise from your grave. Harry Hyams, claim your children.

Pause

Curly You know your way around (*He sits on the ground*).

Jenny (*She sits*) I know them all. Their names. And I wonder about . . .

Curly (*smiling*) The state of their souls.

Jenny (*smiling*) All right.

Pause

Curly I called in on the police when I was getting the car. The railway tickets were first-class. (*Pause*) Can you imagine . . .

Jenny Sarah?

Curly First . . .

Jenny Never. (*Pause*) God. (*Pause*) Have you spoken to him?
Curly Couldn't. (*Pause*) Look at the night.
Jenny Yeah.
Curly Just look at the water.
Jenny You don't want to be like them, Curly.

Curly smiles thinly

Do you? (*Pause*) It's such a beautiful night. Isn't it lovely?
Curly This is the loveliest it gets. (*He gets up and smiles*) I'll take you home. You look wonderful.
Jenny Curly.
Curly Old bean.
Jenny Is that what you say?
Curly What?
Jenny Is that what you say to a girl you want? Old Bean?
Curly Sure.
Jenny I see.
Curly Well . . . (*Pause*) Let's go.
Jenny Curly.
Curly What?
Jenny First-class.
Curly Yes, I know. (*Pause*) It could have been Malloy.
Jenny No. Not his—manner. He would never. Especially with her. She wouldn't allow him.
Curly So.
Jenny So.
Curly I've thought of nothing else.
Jenny Why didn't you ask him?
Curly I will.
Jenny Are you afraid? (*Pause*) That's what I asked you. When we first met.
Curly This place gives me the creeps. (*Pause*) Let's go.
Jenny The essence of pleasure is self-denial. (*She rises, picks up all his clothes and his car-keys and taunts him*)
Curly Oh, Jenny, come on.
Jenny So.
Curly For Christ's sake.

She throws the keys up in the air as a taunt and catches them herse

Jenny Wrap up warm. (*She heads out fast*)
Curly Christ.

Jenny goes out with the keys and clothes

Jenny (*as she goes*) Forget the cold. Listen to Curly . . .
Curly (*bellowing after her*) Patrick's not the only man who travels first-class. (*Pause. Bellowing*) Christ. (*Pause*) Christ. (*Pause. Muttering*)

Christ. (*Pause*) Control yourself. (*Pause*) Control. (*Pause*) I am a pebble.
With self-control. (*Pause. He drops the towel at his feet*)

The Lights fade to a spot on Curly

Eastbourne is a grey city. The lights shine less bright than in L.A. I
wanted to be on the Santa Monica freeway stopping over at Sloppy Joes
for pastrami on rye and one cheese and tomato Anita Ek-burger. I
wanted to be in Caracas paying twenty-five dollars for a Venezualan
sauna. I wanted to be in the Persian mountains playing poker with
Kurd guerillas for lumps of hashish as big as a man's brain. I wanted
to be in that bar in Laos watching that old inverted sphincter puffing and
inhaling, puffing and exhaling: a last inverted monument to human
ingenuity that not even the Americans could bomb into submission.

*The Lights fade and music swells up—"We'll Gather Lilacs"—but not the
thin Lomax version, the full-bodied BBC Concert Orchestra, as—*

the CURTAIN *falls*

INTERVAL

PART II

Scene 9

A Police Station. Day.

Apart from a single flat or cut-out to indicate the setting the stage is bare except for the chair on which Jenny is sitting. A Policeman stands by her.

Policeman Spring of nineteen-twenty-four—April twelfth—a man called Patrick Mahon, lived in London, went to an ironmongers, bought a meat saw and a ten-inch knife. He then went to Waterloo station, collected his suitcase and then took a train to Eastbourne. Waiting in Eastbourne, a Miss Emily Kaye. A young stenographer he had met in London. The idea was to rent a small cottage on the beach to conduct what Mahon referred to as "a love experiment". Miss Kaye had prepared for the experiment by selling some bonds she owned and giving them to Mr Mahon. The cottage they rented was on the stretch of beach known as the Crumbles. They moved in. The experiment lasted three days. On the following Tuesday Mahon strangled her and dismembered her body. He packed some pieces tightly into old boxes and filled biscuit tins with her innards. He attempted to boil down her fat in open saucepans. In the middle of the night, in savage weather, with thunder crashing outside he placed her severed head on the fire. The intense heat of the flames caused the eyes of the dead woman to open. Mahon, a thirty-three-year-old soda fountain salesman, ran from the house. For the first time, horrified. He returned to London. Later he was arrested and executed. (*Pause*) Would anyone in the family have heard that story before?
Jenny Well—Patrick's the most highly educated.

A single cello plays

Scene 10

The Hospital Grounds. Day

Max is discovered, in black, his hands in his pockets. Curly appears, in quite a big overcoat.

Curly Glad you could make it. How was the funeral, Max?
Max Subdued.
Curly Anyone there?

Max Just Malloy's mother.

Curly No-one else?

Max And Jenny.

Curly And Jenny—ah.

Max Yes.

Curly How was that?

Max What?

Curly In black. Did that give you any kind of buzz?

Max Listen . . .

Curly Uh. Ignore it. Proceed. I'd like to hear your alibi for the night Sarah disappeared.

Max It's dull.

Curly I'm sure it's dull. That's not the point.

Max That's a terrible cold you've got.

Curly Now you mention it, yes. I got left out on the beach, you see. Reconstructing the crime. Alibi.

Max I spent the evening with a man called Hart. H-a-r-t. A vet. Well, not a vet exactly. Michael Hart is a spiritualist. He claims that through animals we may talk to the other side.

Curly Go on.

Max The dead. Animals have a psychic flair for communicating with the dead.

Curly I see. So your alibi can be confirmed by a reliable dog.

Max No. No. Confirmed by your father. It was at his house.

Curly Yes?

Max You should talk to him.

Curly just stares at him

It was Sarah's idea. I was working on a series about modern religions. Also Sarah's idea. She loved shopping around. She suggested taking Hart and his famous Alsatian to Patrick's. The idea was she would come with me. I just wanted to get her in the same room as her father. But she funked out—so—I was left with Mr Delafield. He wanted to communicate with his dead wife—your mother. I thought the whole thing was in very bad taste. Patrick was quite serious throughout. Hart's Alsatian kept snarling at him—then fell asleep. Without Sarah the whole exercise was hollow.

Curly She knew you were both there?

Max Oh, yes. She pushed us into it.

Curly And she went off to Eastbourne meanwhile?

Max We later found out. Yes.

Curly Did it occur to you afterwards she could have planned suicide all along and set you two up as a final gag?

Max Yes.

Curly Rather an elaborate gag.

Max Yes.

Curly Muttering away at an Alsatian.

Max But typical.

Curly From what you say.
Max Typical of her.
Curly No longer a nut case?

Max smiles. Pause

Max Check with your father, eh?
Curly Yaar. (*Pause*) As Brigadier-General Bolivar Vallarino of Panama
said to me: "Put it there, pal."

They shake hands

Salut.
Max What's it to be? Tomorrow—same time, same place?
Curly I don't think so, I don't think I want to see you again, Max. Some-
thing of the magic has died.
Max Well, well.

Curly heads out

Abandoning the investigation?
Curly (*turning back*) Thinking about it.
Max That's what your father said you'd do.
Curly Did he say that?
Max He said being back in England made you want a nice job.
Curly I'm looking for an opening certainly.
Max I don't know what arms salesmen usually move on to.
Curly Allied Professions. The Church, you know, the Law. (*He waves*)
Max See you some day.
Curly Not if I see you first. (*He sings*)
                    "Keep young and beautiful
                     It's your duty to be beautiful
                     Keep young and beautiful
                     If you want to be loved."

The Lights fade to Black-Out

SCENE II

The Shadow of the Moon bar. Night.

*In the darkness, Max follows on immediately with Curly's song from the
previous scene*

Max   "Keep young and beautiful
                     It's your duty to be beautiful
                     Keep young and beautiful
                     If you want to be loved . . ."

The Lights come up on the bar scene. Jenny is discovered behind the bar. She turns as she hears the singing. Max dances on

Jenny I thought you were Curly.

Max What I say is: the world is a rice pudding. It's just waiting to be skinned.

Jenny You've met him too?

Max Oh yes. My dear.

Jenny The bar's closed.

Max Nice place. Where's the people?

Jenny Gone home.

Max Scotch.

Jenny Max. You look funny without her.

Max I feel funny. No longer the parrot on the shoulder. I get through whole sentences without interruption . . .

Jenny I warned you . . .

Max What?

Jenny That she'd kill herself.

Max Oh that?

Jenny That.

Pause

Max Scotch.

Jenny I think she said, Max I'm going to kill myself. And you said just show me. And she did. (*Pause*) How many times did I tell you?

Max Often. You leapt at the opportunity.

Jenny I was pointing out . . .

Max You did best all round.

Jenny What do you mean?

Max This place. You win the Shadow of the Moon.

Pause

Jenny I see.

Max Well, so you're happy.

Jenny Max.

Max Now the lover is buried.

Jenny He was not my lover.

Max He just left you the club.

Jenny It was nothing to do with it.

Max Tell that to Mrs Malloy.

Jenny Malloy married . . .

Max Malloy's mother. At the funeral. Mrs Malloy.

Pause

Jenny What are you talking about?

Max I have a photo of you in a gymslip. (*He steps behind the bar to Jenny*) With a straw hat and black socks.

Jenny What about Mrs Malloy?

Max This is a knife. Kiss me. (*Pause*) Hands behind head.

She does so

Now follow me out from behind the bar.

They come out. We see the knife

Sit down. Keep your hands there.

She sits down. He sits opposite

I sit myself down. Don't move.

The knife is held by Max for the scene

There aren't many girls left in Guildford.

Jenny No.

Max Speak up.

Jenny I said no, not many.

Max What with Juliet. And Fizz and Laura gone now. And the other Laura. And Jane Hammond got passed down the line. And the one with the lisp. They tell me Alice has been had by most of the Bank of England . . .

Jenny So I hear.

Max Sally and Pip . . .

Jenny Yes . . .

Max Both to chartered accountants, inevitably. Gloria, married. Janice. I'm scraping the very bottom of the barrel. Tamara. That doesn't leave many. Any. Of the ones who used to come here. And the ones who didn't come here were rubbish. Sarah would do anything you wanted. (*Pause*) Rather a disgusting characteristic. (*Pause*) Penny on her seventh actor and Jacqueline a nun. That leaves you. Oh, Jenny. What happens to people?

Jenny I don't know.

Max When we came here as teenagers—you and me and Sarah—you never knew what would happen. It seemed the most ambiguous place in the world. Like falling into satin in the dark. And look at it now. (*Pause*) Tell me what you think of Curly. (*Pause*) You know he's given up looking for Sarah already.

Jenny I didn't know that.

Max He's everything the world wasn't going to be. Blustering. And sneering. And insincere. Is that really what you want?

Jenny Then put the knife away.

Max Do you really want Curly?

Jenny He's never touched me, Max. (*Pause*) Tell me about Mrs Malloy.

Max Do you really know nothing? (*Pause*) She's in hospital. She may not have been mad when she went in. But she's certainly mad now. Jennifer. (*Pause*) I find your innocence unforgivable. (*Pause*) Take off your clothes.

Nothing

Lie down on the floor.

Nothing

Close your eyes, open your mouth, praise the Lord and thank God you're British. (*Pause*) Goodnight.

Max goes out immediately, putting the knife away

The Lights change

Jenny Young women in Guildford must expect to be threatened. Men here lead ugly lives and girls are the only touchstones left. Cars cruise beside you as you walk down the pavement, I have twice been attacked at the country club, the man in the house opposite has a telephoto lens, my breasts are often touched on commuter trains, my body is covered with random thumbprints, the doctor says he needs to undress me completely to vaccinate my arm, men often spill drinks in my lap, or brush cigarettes against my bottom, very old men bump into me and clutch at my legs as they fall. I have been offered drinks, money, social advancement and once an editorial position on the *Financial Times*. I expect this to go on. I expect to be bumped, bruised, followed, assaulted, stared at and propositioned for the rest of my life, while at the same time offering sanctuary, purity, reassurance, prestige—the only point of loveliness in men's ever-darkening lives.

SCENE 12

Guildford Railway Station. Night

Jenny is sitting on a bench reading a newspaper. A Porter and Curly enter from opposite sides. Curly has a briefcase and umbrella

Jenny Well. You're getting very hard to find.
Curly Get my luggage, will you? And a taxi.
Porter Sir.

The Porter goes out

Jenny (*allowing nothing*) They tell me your heart's gone out of it. The investigation.
Curly Can't do it all the time.
Jenny Even thinking of a job. Insurance. Something like Lloyd's.
Curly Well I've been up to town. Just to talk it over.
Jenny Costs a lot of money.
Curly Seventy-five thousand entrance fee. That's all a chap needs. Buy himself a slice of security.

Jenny (*lethally*) I brought you the keys to your car.

Jenny throws the keys over. Curly catches them, embarrassed

Little man.

Curly (*smiling*) Jenny.

Jenny And some information. (*Pause*) I've been to see a Mrs Malloy. She's seventy-three. Initials E. R. Malloy. As, she said, like the Queen. Am I keeping you?

Curly No, no.

Jenny Malloy's mother lived in one house for the whole of her life. A Victorian house in the centre of Guildford. Married for a month in nineteen-eighteen before her husband was killed at Chemin des Dames. At the age of sixty-eight she transferred the house into her son's name. Tax dodge: you avoid death duties. Standard practice round here. She put it in her son's name. But she went on living there herself. So. Central Guildford. Torn apart as you know. And some developers bought the rest of the block. It tempted Malloy. He held the deeds. There was only one obstacle. His mother had lived there the whole of her life. He held out for a couple of months. Then suddenly cracked. He had her committed.

Curly Was she mad?

Jenny Oh, Curly, come on.

Curly Was she mad?

Jenny She was mad when enough people needed her to be. Let's face it. She was pushed. Malloy signed the committal order.

Curly Is there any actual evidence she was pushed?

Jenny Oh, Curly . . .

Curly How much did he make?

Jenny Two hundred thousand.

Pause

Curly She was pushed.

Jenny (*rising*) And another property thrown in. A run-down old barn on the other side of town. A nightclub called the Shadow of the Moon. Mrs Malloy in the mental hospital sent her nurse on an errand. The nurse was Sarah. Where the old woman's house had been she found seventeen floors of prestige offices crowned with an antique supermarket. She went back to the hospital. Everyone should know everything. That's what she said. She told the old woman her house had gone. If she wasn't mad before, she certainly is now. (*Pause*) Sarah was electrified when she found out. No wonder she rowed with Malloy. Can you imagine? Her friend Malloy—one of life's losers turns out to be a shark. She would have flipped. She would have told everyone. But the amazing thing is: she didn't. For the first time in her life she kept something secret. From me, from everyone. Except Max. Max was a journalist. He would have said what a wonderful story. Stockbroker swindles his own Mother in Property Deal. But the story never appeared.

I think he went to Malloy and blackmailed him. (*Pause*) Do you want to go back to London?

Curly How do you know all this?

Jenny Partly from Max.

Curly Did he tell you?

Jenny He . . .

Curly What?

Jenny Signalled he knew.

Curly How?

Jenny With a knife. He came to the club last night. He thought I knew . . .

Curly What made him think that?

Jenny Because Malloy was in love with me, that's why he left the Shadow of the Moon to me. Max thought it was because Malloy was my lover . . .

Curly Whereas in fact . . .

Jenny It was because he was never my lover.

Curly Yes. That makes perfect sense round here. So if Max did blackmail Malloy you're saying he only had one problem . . .

Jenny The old problem we have met before.

Curly How to close Sarah's mouth.

Jenny Sarah will want to know why Max hasn't published the story.

Curly God . . .

Jenny How to shut her up . . .

Curly What a beautiful girl this Sarah is. Niagra. Vesuvius. Grinding on against injustice and the misery of the world.

Jenny Max's only problem . . .

Curly Yaaar.

Pause

Jenny Is that what happened?

Curly Why take her to the Crumbles?

Jenny Because in nineteen-twenty-four there was a particularly disgusting murder there.

Curly Well exactly . . .

Jenny What?

Curly Why draw attention to yourself? The Crumbles. The worst possible place. It's the Wembley Stadium of murder already.

Jenny (*quietly*) Right.

Pause. Curly turns and looks at her. Dead quiet, please

Curly What do you mean he had a knife?

Jenny I've just said it.

Curly Tell me.

Jenny shakes her head

  What happened?

Jenny Why should I?

Curly Jenny.

Jenny He never came near.

Curly Jenny. (*Pause*) I'm not telling you the truth.

Jenny I wouldn't expect it.

Curly I don't like to be honest. It's not in my nature.

Jenny (*smiling*) Go on.

Curly I'd heard a bit about Malloy, not about his mother, that surprises me, but about his house. You see on a crooked deal a blackmailer will have a choice of targets. Malloy. Or the property company. Or the man who finances the property company. That old Victorian house? Patrick's money bought it.

Pause

Jenny Max blackmails Patrick . . .

Curly Congratulations.

Jenny Max gets rid of Sarah, then forces Patrick into confirming his ludicrous alibi about the dog.

Curly You're very quick. (*Pause*) They seem to have lost my luggage.

Jenny Which one will you go for first?

Curly You're very keen.

Jenny You getting frightened, Curly? Is that what it is? Losing your nerve. Frightened to hurt your father? Frightened to face up to him?

Curly Face up to Spats.

Jenny What luggage?

Curly All my things. I'm moving down here. Get a job. Get a house. I like the atmosphere. (*Pause*) Don't stare at me, kid. (*Pause*) Listen, the story's ridiculous. It's full of holes. If Max went to blackmail my father, he would have just said he didn't know . . .

Jenny But for the property company conning an old woman is bad publicity . . .

Curly It happens all the time. It's called business practice, people go to the wall.

Jenny Nobody would believe them.

Curly They'd say they didn't know. It's just a matter of keeping your nerve and a plausible story . . .

Jenny Who's to say it's plausible?

Curly Exactly. Newspapers can be bought, judges can be leant on, politicians can be stuffed with truffles and cognac. Life's a racket, that we know.

Jenny Christ, I'll make a person of you yet.

Curly Forget it. (*Pause*) Listen—sugar plum—the horror of the world. The horror of the world is there are no excuses left. There was a time when men who ruined other men, could claim they were ignorant or simple or believed in God, or life was very hard, or we didn't know what we were doing, but now everybody knows the tricks, the same shabby hands have been played over and over, and men who persist in old ways of running their countries or their lives, those men now do it in the full knowledge of what they're doing. So that at last greed and selfishness and cruelty stand exposed in white neon: men are bad because they want to be. No excuses left.

Jenny You mean you're not going to see him?

Curly (*smiling*) No, I'm not.

Jenny Well, why not just say that? (*Pause*) Like to have known you better, Curly.

The Porter wheels on Curly's luggage, a huge Singapore trunk.
  Jenny goes out

Porter Here she is, sir. (*Pause*) Moving down here, are you, sir?

Curly No. Change of plan. Left luggage. Twenty-four hours.

Curly heads off

"*We'll Gather Lilacs*" *is heard, Lomax-style*

SCENE 13

The Shadow of the Moon bar. Night.

The Barman is alone behind his bar. Curly walks in, vicious, drunk and smoking.

Curly Give me a Scotch.

Barman Right away, sir.

Curly And don't be so bloody pleasant.

Barman Sir.

Curly Now go upstairs, knock politely on her door and tell her there's something slimy to see her. (*He takes the bottle and glass*)

Barman Sir.

The Barman goes out

Curly (*shouting*) For God's sake, Lomax, give us all a break. Just shut up.

"*We'll Gather Lilacs*" *stumbles and stops*

(*Sitting at the table*) Not as if anyone was dancing up there. Just looks like the bloody *Titanic*.

The Barman returns

Barman She says . . .

Curly Yes, Barman?

Barman She says. Piss off. Sir.
Curly White-knickered do-good cock-shrivelling cow.
Barman She wants you to go, sir.
Curly Want to make something of it, Barman? (*He threatens the Barman with the bottle*)
Barman Sir.
Curly I'm glad I didn't sell you a gun.
Jenny (*off*) Mike. Get scraping.

Curly turns at the strips

Curly Down I go.

Curly exits

Lomax (*off*) Come on, everybody. Let's Bossa Nova.
The Lomax Band plays a Bossa Nova.

SCENE 14

The Hospital Grounds. Night.

Max is tapping his knife, unopened, against his hand. After a moment Curly appears, in a big overcoat.

Curly Hullo, Max.
Max Hullo.
Curly I'm sorry to drag you out here in the middle of the night.
Max That's all right.
Curly At barely ten minutes' notice.
Max That's all right.
Curly No, it's not. You should be angry. (*Pause*) You're an innocent party. Act angry. (*Pause*) Story is you *murdered* Sarah. We don't believe that, do we, Max? We don't think you're the murdering type.

Max flashes his flick knife out

(*Quickly taking out his gun*) Every man has his own gun. That's not a metaphor. That's a fact. Only some have more guns than others. Knife.

Max hands his knife to Curly

I have a bottle in my pocket. Remove it.

Max tenderly takes the bottle from Curly's pocket

And put it down there.

Max puts it on the ground

And stay down. (*Hard and fast*) I think you took money, Max. That
was your crime. It's not the local custom, I have observed. In England
they don't take money. They make money. Spot the difference. It's a
country of opportunity. Everyone can run a racket of their own. Say I
discover some property developers have used unusual pressures to
achieve their aims. I don't go and ask for a share of their money. I go
out and find a defenceless old cow of my own to swindle. That is the
creative thing to do.

Max I'd never taken money before.

Curly I don't care. Your back is snapped. From now till the millenium.
They have your number. (*Pause*) Have a drink.

Max No, thank you.

Curly Have a drink.

Max takes a swig

I don't think you have it in you to kill. But, Christ, you have it in you
to wheedle. Have another drink.

Max takes a swig

Sarah told you about the deal. You were to investigate. But you didn't
go to Malloy. You went to Patrick. For cash. I have one question. Why
did Patrick consent?

Max shrugs

Please don't lie to me, Max. Have another drink.

Max drinks again

Pretend you're Malloy.

Max drinks again

Why did Patrick give you the money?

Max He . . .

Curly Have another drink.

Max drinks again

Why did Patrick bother? He should have kept his nerve. He had a perfectly plausible story . . .

Max He . . .

Curly Drink.

Max drinks again

Have a cigarette.

Curly throws down a cigarette and a box of matches. Max lights up

He could have said he never knew. Is that not what people say? In such
circumstances.

Max He . . .

Curly Drink.

Max drinks again

I understand he arranged the bridging loan for the building. He would barely have been implicated.
Max There . . .
Curly Drink.

Max drinks again

It's a half-baked sort of scandal that I can't quite understand. That's why I'm asking for your help. Have another cigatette.

Max lights a second cigarette, then lights two for Curly. Curly sticks one in Max's nose and one in Max's right ear

Drink.

Max drinks, coughs and splutters and drops the cigarettes

You're just about ready to tell me the truth.
Max They put a dog in . . .
Curly Dog?
Max Hart . . .
Curly The spiritualist . . .
Max Yes. Uses his dogs for other purposes . . .
Curly The ones that talk to the dead?
Max Can also be hired out on eviction jobs.
Curly But Malloy sold up.
Max Not at first. He wouldn't be bought. So they decided to flush him out of the house. Mrs Malloy was at the cinema. Malloy was alone. Hart stole the fuses. Then put an Alsatian in.
Curly What happened?
Max Malloy blew it apart with a shotgun.
Curly God almighty.
Max He did it in the dark. It was the fight of his life. He knew it was Hart's, he phoned him. I'm going to be sick.
Curly Don't—be sick. That means Patrick wasn't there that night. And it wasn't his dog. And it's not even publicly his profit. You had nothing on him. Why did he pay?
Max I had something on him. I had Sarah on him. He was terrified she'd find out that he was behind it. He was thinking of Sarah. He paid up. He loved her.
Curly Mistake.
Max On the last day—Sarah found out. It had been—it had been . . .
Curly Like holding Niagara . . .
Max Yes . . .
Curly Everyone should know everything.
Max Yes.
Curly How did she take it?
Max She was possessed. She'd killed a dog before.
Curly Yes.

Max When she was a child.
Curly Yes.
Max She kept saying: what happens to dogs.
Curly What happens to dogs.
Max What happens to people.

Pause

Curly Finish the bottle.
Max I . . .
Curly Finish.

Max drinks again. Curly makes him finish; then bangs down his fist on the end; then gets up

Now get up.
Max I can't.
Curly Take your empties. And go.

Max crawls off

Curly stamps put the cigarette ends. The Lights change

So it came back to Spats. It would always come back to Spats. The world is not run by innocents or small men who happen to believe the wrong thing. It is run by uncomfortably large, obscenely quiet men called Spats. The time was coming when I'd have to face Patrick. Patrick was no longer perfect. I had found a way in. In the thick, densely carpeted air of a merchant bank, the sound of a slight scuffle and the warm red smell of dog. Glimpsed for a second the implausible face of a man who loved his own daughter. I was in.

Music starts.

SCENE 15

The Delafields' drawing-room. Night.

Curly is sitting in his overcoat with his feet up, waiting. The door opens and Patrick comes in, bleary-eyed, in dressing-gown and pyjamas.

Patrick Curly.
Curly Happy birthday, Spats.
Patrick Did you just wake me up?
Curly Come in. Sit down.
Patrick What's happened?
Curly You're O.K. Sit down.

Patrick sits

Patrick I'd like a glass of hot water.
Curly Not yet.

Patrick gets his little box out

Put your eyes in. Attaboy.

Patrick leans back and dabs contact lenses on to his eyes

Can you see me now?
Patrick Yes.
Curly I have my fingers on your throat. Feel anything? There's been a development. Stray dog. About a year ago. You were avoiding a public enquiry, I should think. Irreparable damage to the character of Guildford. So someone decided to flush out Malloy.
Patrick Well?
Curly Well?
Patrick I know what you're talking about. And I didn't condone their methods. Stupid. I was appalled.
Curly You didn't know at the time?
Patrick I run a merchant bank. I sanctioned the purchase—not the method of purchase.
Curly But he brought you the corpse.
Patrick The dead dog? Yes. He left it on my doorstep. A tuppenny gesture.
Curly How did he know that you were behind it?
Patrick He worked in the City. Remember. He could fight his way through. He knew the routes.
Curly But why did he sell? After he'd blown the dog apart. It was his victory. Why did he not seize it?

Pause

Patrick Why do people give in? Because they recognize the way things are. He had made his point. He'd planted his tiny flag on the hillside and now—well, if you saw the site—there was just this old Victorian house, alone among the rubble of a demolition site. You looked at it. It was aching to come down. It had to.
Curly I don't understand.
Patrick Think. Even after that night, to hold on to the house would have meant turning your life into a battlefield, a constant act of self-assertion. Nobody wants to live like that. Straining endlessly to make your point. And why? He already had the moral victory. I glimpsed his face the following morning on the eight-thirty-three. He looked up at me. A pleasurable glow of self-righteousness—the fight of his life and he'd won . . .
Curly Weren't you ashamed?
Patrick He had the righteousness. I had the house. (*Pause*) Peace with honour. That is the phrase. It means surrender. But of a very special

kind. With the sweet heart of your integrity intact. (*Pause*) He had that. I had—well, so far it's nudging into its third million . . .

Curly This moral victory—the fight of his life . . .

Patrick Yes?

Curly Wasn't much use in his dying year.

Patrick That wasn't my fault. Peace with honour—peace with shame. It's a very thin line. A matter of believing—your own propaganda. (*Pause*) And all for a girl.

Curly Everyone loves Jenny.

Pause

Patrick Stick to your story I used to say. When I met Malloy later in the street. In the last days of alcoholic collapse. I told him. Stick to your story. You killed the dog. You revealed my corruption. Great victory. Old man. (*Pause*) Curly. Life is pain. Pure and simple. Pain. Around. Below. All pain. But we have a choice. Either to protest noisily—to scream against the pain, to rattle and wail—or else—to submerge that pain, to channel it . . . (*Pause*) Preferably in someone else's direction. (*Pause*) If I admitted everything that had happened in my life, laid it out in a field like that contents of an air disaster, would it really help?

Curly Go back to Sarah.

Patrick No.

Curly Everyone should know everything? That's what I believe.

Patrick Very well.

Curly You went to Max.

Patrick Not at all. He came to us. Saying he knew about Mrs Malloy. We had nothing to fear . . .

Curly You'd have kept your nerve.

Patrick I should hope so . . .

Curly And a plausible story.

Patrick He said he knew about the dog. Again it was nothing. We could have denied all knowledge.

Curly In fact you do.

Patrick Oh, yes. (*Pause*) Of course. We sent him away. It was rubbish. But as an afterthought he said he'd tell Sarah. (*Pause*) Curly. You may not believe it. The City of London once enjoyed a reputation for unimpeachable integrity. My word is my bond. So fabulously wealthy as to be almost beyond wealth. But in the last twenty years we've been dragged through the mud like everyone else. The wide boys and the profiteers have sullied our reputation. We work now like stallholders against a barrage of abuse. (*Pause*) Who is to set standards? Curly. Who is to lead? You have to be able to believe—my daughter should not be given the chance to doubt—we were honest men . . . (*Pause*) We are honest men. She had always abused me. But she had never been able to fault me. (*Pause*) I had to buy Dupree. Do you understand? For her sake.

Curly smiles

Curly How did you buy him?

Patrick A package. Rather lurid. I got him—a job in London, and a series of leads on my younger, less scrupulous colleagues, gave him a little money . . .

Curly Is that all?

Patrick No. We negotiated.

Curly What?

Patrick A large anonymous donation to an anarchist party of his own choosing. (*Pause*) On those terms he could take it. Do you see?

Curly Go on.

Patrick That was it.

Curly Apart from Sarah.

Patrick Apart from Sarah that was it. (*Pause*) Sarah. Unquenchable. A deep well of unhappiness down which I could have thrown anarchist subscriptions, dead dogs, pints of my own warm blood, I could have turned on my head, destroyed my own life, and still she would not have been satisfied. (*Pause*) Like you. (*Pause*) The two of you. Like woodpeckers. Nothing will stop you. In her case it was pity for the world. In yours . . .

Curly Go on.

Patrick In yours . . .

Curly Go on.

Patrick Disgust. (*Pause*) You have a beady little heart, Curly. It pumps away. I've watched. One thing fires you. The need to ensure everyone is as degraded as you are.

Pause

Curly Go on.

Patrick Max was like the rest of us. He got worn down. By the endless wanting to know. Now she wanted to know why the story had never appeared. (*Pause*) He told her. Your father is financing the building. I have been paid off. Malloy was paid off. A dog is dead. Everyone should know everything. She went mad. (*Pause*) The dog in particular. She was obsessed with the dog. She went straight to Victoria. I followed as soon as I could. (*Pause*) I got into Eastbourne at midnight. The last train down. It was too late to try all the hotels. I went down to the promenade. By the silver railings there was a girl in a light-coloured raincoat. She had black frizzy hair. It was dark and drizzling and I couldn't see. She was squatting down. As I got nearer I could see she was pissing. On the promenade. She finished. She got up. And her coat was open. She was wearing nothing underneath. It was raining and it was very cold. She just wandered away. (*Pause*) That's Eastbourne beach. (*Pause*) I started to follow her. I had no choice.

Curly What did she say?

Patrick She said nothing.

Curly Go on.

Patrick We walked. A procession of two, through acres of bungalows to the open land. A flat rocky patch stretching away to the sea. The distance between us religiously observed. (*Pause*) She sat down on the concrete jetty. (*Pause*) Those who wish to reform the world should first know a little bit about it. I told her some stories of life in the City—the casual cruelty of each day; take-over bids, redundancies, men ruined overnight, jobs lost, trusts betrayed, reputations smashed, life in that great trough called the City of London, sploshing about in the cash. And I asked, what I have always asked: how will that ever change?

Curly Tell me of any society that has not operated in this way.

Patrick Five years after a revolution . . .

Curly The shit rises . . .

Patrick The same pattern . . .

Curly The weak go to the wall . . .

Patrick Somebody's bound to get hurt . . .

Curly You can't make omelettes . . .

Patrick The pursuit of money is a force for progress . . .

Curly It's always been the same . . .

Patrick The making of money . . .

Curly The breaking of men.

Patrick The two together. Always. The sound of progress.

Curly The making of money. The breaking of men.

Pause

Patrick If I didn't do it . . .

Curly Somebody else would. (*Pause*) And what did she say?

Patrick She said nothing. (*Pause*) Finally, after twenty-one years she said nothing. Wrapped the mac tighter about her body. (*Pause*) We watched the dawn. If I'd moved towards the jetty she would have thrown herself in. At five-thirty she was calm. She still said nothing. I took the decision. I walked into the town. I rang Hart from the *Cavendish* and told him to come and collect her. Then I got a train up to town.

Curly What?

Patrick I had a meeting. (*Pause*) Money. (*Pause*) Hart arrived to look after her at a quarter past seven. He was to drive her back. He followed my instructions to the beach. She was gone. Her raincoat was on the jetty. It was the only article of clothing she'd been wearing. It's safe to say she killed herself. (*Pause*) The suicide was calculated from the start. Not uncommon. She had challenged Max to make me come to Eastbourne. Two malicious gestures. She had chosen to die at a place famous for a ghastly murder. And second, she had left two first-class tickets behind. The clearest possible way of saying—someone else is involved. (*Pause*) It was me. (*Pause*) She had to bang down her flag. Like everyone else.

Curly How do I know this is true? (*He rises*) For all I know, you travelled down with her. You could have killed her.

Patrick Is that what you think?

Pause

Curly No. I believe you absolutely. The story has just the right amount of quiet. She slipped obligingly into the sea. An English murder. Who needs ropes or guns or daggers? We can trust our victims to pass quietly in the night. Slip way into the bottle. Or the looney bin. Just—fall away with barely the crack of a knuckle as they go. (*Pause*) I'm sure she died on the beach. I'm sure that you—were sixty miles away.

Patrick I didn't go to the police. I rigged up the alibi with Hart and Dupree.

Curly You left her to die.

Patrick No, that's what the police would have said.

Curly That's what you did.

Patrick It was a knife-edge decision. In the morning light. To stay or go. I had to decide which was better. Then something she said made up my mind for me.

Curly She spoke.

Patrick Just once.

Curly What did she say?

Patrick A single thing. "What I despise most," she said, "is your pretence to be civilized." (*Pause*) I was reassured. The same old propaganda. The noise of someone who's going to live. The same old drivel. She was bleating again. So I left . . .

Curly In fact . . .

Patrick In fact she meant it. (*Pause*) And that is the nail on which my life is hung. She meant it. (*Pause*) But I see no reason to drag it out in public.

Curly Sure . . .

Patrick If I wish to continue . . .

Curly Making money . . .

Patrick The facts must be suppressed. The girl is dead. It makes no difference now.

Pause

Curly I possess a lethal combination of facts. Suppose I go to the press? The old woman, the dog, abandoning your daughter on the beach . . .

Patrick (*calling*) Mrs Dunning. (*To Curly*) You let it out. You ruin me. He left his daughter to kill herself. A despicable thing to do. Bad publicity. I leave my job. What happens? Someone else pops up in my place. Life covers up pretty fast. Only the people bleed. (*Calling*) Mrs Dunning. (*To Curly*) Both of you did well. You wrung from me the same confession. You wanted me to say I was degraded. Well . . . (*Pause*) I am. (*Pause*) O.K.? So now can I please go back to work?

Mrs Dunning comes in, also in a dressing-gown

Mrs Dunning You must be quiet, Pat.

Patrick I'm sorry.

Mrs Dunning You must stay calm. You'd better go to bed.

Patrick I'm sorry.

Mrs Dunning That's all right. You'll be fine.

Curly I just want to say . . .

Mrs Dunning Sssh. Be quiet. Come to bed.
Curly Let me say . . .
Mrs Dunning Sssh. Quiet please. Let's everyone be quiet. (*Pause*) All right,
Pat? (*She smiles and kisses Pat on the cheek*)
Patrick My darling.
Mrs Dunning Good night.
Patrick Good night.

Patrick goes out

Mrs Dunning (*at the door*) And we'll try to forget you were ever disturbed.

Mrs Dunning goes out

Curly is left alone. The Lights change

Curly Under the random surface of events lie steel-grey explanations. The
more unlikely and implausible the facts, the more rigid the obscene
geometry below. I was holding my father's life in my hands. I had to
make up my mind. If I ditched my father, told the newspapers the story
of those days, all I would be doing would be to bang down my tiny
flag on the same mountain-side as Sarah. Somewhere every so often
in this world there will appear this tiny little weed called morality. It will
push up quietly through the tarmac and there my father will be waiting
with a cement grinder and a shovel to concrete it over. It is inadequate.
It cannot help us now. There are no excuses left. Two sides. Two sides
only. Lloyd's of London was beckoning me. I could feel its soft fiscal
embrace. I wanted its quiet and its surety. I would sit in Lloyd's and wait
for the end. I lay back. But I wanted Jenny beside me. I wanted to rest
my head between her legs. I was ready to chase the same shadow, to
tread the same path as Dupree and Malloy: all of us after the same one
thing: the hard, bright, glistening girl who ran the Shadow of the Moon.

Music, "We'll Gather Lilacs", very loud.

SCENE 16

The Shadow of the Moon bar. Night.
Jenny is in the bar. As the music stops, Curly enters.

Curly Come for a quick one.
Jenny Come in.
Curly Bet I'm the worse soak you ever had.

Jenny smiles and gets him a bottle

You're up pretty early.
Jenny Yes. Do you want some breakfast?
Curly I . . .

Jenny looks up

I talked to Patrick.
Jenny What did he say?
Curly He knew nothing. It turned out.
Jenny You mean . . . ?
Curly He really is completely innocent.
Jenny What about Malloy?
Curly That was—quite another business.
Jenny I see.
Curly Nothing to do with it. Or with Patrick. He didn't know.
Jenny Why did she kill herself?
Curly Well . . . (*Pause*) You said it. She was paranoid. I think she got
depressed.
Jenny Nothing to do with Malloy . . .
Curly No.
Jenny Or Patrick.
Curly No.
Jenny I see.
Curly She just wasn't quite cut out for things.
Jenny No . . .
Curly Looking back. Inevitable. You understand.
Jenny Oh, yes.

Pause

Curly Some people. You can see it coming.
Jenny I got a letter this morning. Shall I read it to you?
Curly Please.

Jenny takes out a sheet, leans against the bar, reads

Jenny "My darlings, whoops that's fig juice if you're wondering.
Let us rejoice in the ugliness of the world. Strangely I am not upset. I
am reassured. I think I left a finger pointing on the beach.
Jenny, keep Pat on the flat of his back. On his knees. Keep him con-
fessing. Keep the wound fresh.
I walked five miles before I found any clothes.
Insist we are degraded.
Resist all those who tell you otherwise.
At all costs fight innocence.
Forbid ignorance.
Startle your children.
Appal your mothers.
Know everything.
Love everything.
Especially—

Decay.

Insist on decay.

I have twice been debauched in the open road. I am travelling at this moment through France. Don't tell Pat.

Good-bye, sweet friends, good-bye."

Pause

I think it's from her. I don't know anyone else . . . (*Pause*) He called me up.

Curly Who?

Jenny Patrick.

Curly What did he say?

Jenny He said . . . (*Pause*) Don't look so worried.

Curly (*smiling*) No, no . . .

Jenny This was yesterday.

Curly Ah.

Jenny He said he'd like to buy this place.

Curly Here?

Jenny Yeah.

Curly What did you say?

Jenny He's offering a very good price.

Curly I'm sure.

Jenny It's a crummy sort of building as you can see.

Curly Yeah . . .

Jenny You know . . .

Curly Yeah.

Jenny Some whisky stains and a few tears . . .

Curly Jenny . . .

Jenny I said no.

Pause

Curly Jenny . . .

Jenny So . . .

Curly Oh, Jenny . . .

Pause

Jenny Thanks for your help.

Curly What?

Jenny Sarah.

Curly Well . . .

Jenny Thank you. (*Pause*) I had a long talk with Michael Hart. About Malloy. And the dog. And Patrick's behaviour on the beach. (*Pause*) I know everything. (*Pause*) So do you.

Pause

Curly Keep your chin up

Jenny And you.

Curly (*backing away*) I liked your legs. I've always liked your legs.

Jenny Good-bye.

Curly Good-bye.

Jenny goes out

The Lights change

Why should I feel ashamed of myself? Why should I feel inferior? Why should I feel anything? Jenny would go to the newspaper. They didn't believe her. And, anyway, Sarah was alive. It was autumn again. In the mean square mile of the City of London they were making money. (*Smiling*) Back to my guns.

The Lights fade

CURTAIN

FURNITURE AND PROPERTY LIST

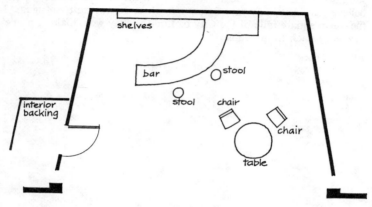

PART I

SCENE 1

On stage: Bar and shelves. *On them:* various drinks, including lemonade and
whisky, glasses, measures (one with blotting-paper wad), ashtrays,
lemons in dish, general dressing
2 bar stools
2 chairs
Table. *On it:* drink for Jenny, ashtray, matches

Personal: **Jenny:** cigarette
Curly: cigarettes

SCENE 2

On stage: Sofa
Armchair
Coffee-table. *On it:* suitcase open with clothes in it
Shelves. *On them:* photo of Sarah in frame, dressing
On floor by table: box of girl's clothes, etc., including gymslip, Alice
band, exercise book

Off stage: Tray with 2 cups, 2 saucers, 2 spoons, teapot, milk jug, sugar bowl,
plate of cakes and walnut whips (**Mrs Dunning**)

Personal: **Patrick:** watch

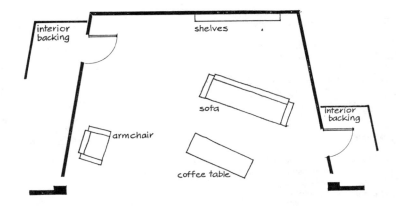

SCENE 3

On stage: Nil

Off stage: Rack of rifles and loaded revolver (**Storeman**)

Personal: **Curley:** wad of money

SCENE 4

On stage: Bench

SCENE 5

On stage: Furniture as Scene 2
             On coffee-table: open music score
             On shelves: bottle of whisky, glasses, other drinks as dressing

Personal: **Curly:** packet of tipped cigarettes, packet of plain cigarettes, 2 cigars,
             packet of sweets, packet of condoms

SCENE 6

On stage: Furniture as Scene 1
             On bar: damp cloth, dirty ashtray
             Under bar: rubbish bin, magazines
             On shelves: jug of lemonade, glass, bottle of whisky, glass
             On table: glass of whisky, cigarettes, matches, ashtray

Personal: **Jenny:** handkerchief

SCENE 7

On stage: Furniture as Scene 2
          On shelf: replace whisky bottle
          In armchair: crochet work
          On coffee-table: book

Personal: **Patrick:** car keys

SCENE 8

On stage: Nil

Off stage: Duffel coat and sweater (**Jenny**)
          Curly's sweater and slacks, with car keys in pocket
          Towel (**Jenny**)
Personal: **Curly:** paper bag

PART II

SCENE 9

On stage: Chair

SCENE 10

On stage: Furniture as Scene 4

SCENE 11

On stage: Furniture as Scene 1
          On table: dirty ashtray
          On bar: 4 dirty glasses, dish of cocktail "bits", tea towel, damp cloth,
            ashtray

Personal: **Max:** flick knife

SCENE 12

On stage: Bench. *On it:* newspaper

Off stage: Briefcase, umbrella (**Curly**)
          Trolley with large trunk (**Porter**)

SCENE 13

On stage: Furniture as Scene 1
               On table: ashtray
               On shelves: jug of lemonade, bottle of whisky, glass
               On bar: dish with lemons, knife

SCENE 14

On stage: Furniture as Scene 4

Off stage: Gun in holster (**Curly**)
            Bottle of whisky (**Curly**)

Personal: **Curly:** 4 cigarettes, matches

SCENE 15

On stage: Furniture as Scene 2

Personal: **Patrick:** contact lenses box

SCENE 16

On stage: Furniture as Scene 1
               On shelf: bottle of whisky, glass
               On bar: ashtray

Off stage: Letter (**Jenny**)

LIGHTING PLOT

NOTE: Lighting cues are given as indicated in the text: if preferred, set changes can be done in black-outs instead of curtain drops, and cues inserted at the end of each Scene

Property fittings required: nil
5 interior, 2 exterior settings

PART I

SCENE 1. Night
To open: General interior lighting for Club Bar
No cues

SCENE 2. Night
To open: Warm interior lighting for Drawing-room
No cues

SCENE 3. Day
To open: General lighting for Warehouse interior
No cues

SCENE 4. Day
To open: Black-Out except for spot on **Curly**

Cue 1   **Curly**: "Pinpricks."   (Page 13)
         Bring up general lighting for exterior of Hospital Grounds

SCENE 5. Night
To open: As Scene 2
No cues

SCENE 6. Night
To open: As Scene 1
No cues

SCENE 7. Night
To open: As Scene 2
No cues

Knuckle   59

SCENE 8. Night

To open: Night lighting on bare stage to suggest lonely beach

Cue 2   **Curly:** "With self-control."   (Page 30)
            General fade to spot on Curly

Cue 3   **Curly:** ". . . bomb into submission."   (Page 30)
            Fade to Black-Out

                              PART II

SCENE 9. Day

To open: Cold interior lighting

No cues

SCENE 10. Day

To open: As Scene 4

No cues

SCENE 11. Night

To open: Black-Out

Cue 4   As **Max** enters   (Page 34)
            Fade up to Scene 1 lighting

Cue 5   **Max** exits   (Page 36)
            Fade to spot on Jenny

SCENE 12. Night

To open: Effect of gloomy railway station lighting

No cues

SCENE 13. Night

To open: As Scene 1

No cues

SCENE 14. Night

To open: Dim exterior lighting

Cue 6   **Max** exits   (Page 44)
            Fade to spot on Curly

SCENE 15. Night

To open: As Scene 2

Cue 7   **Mrs Dunning** exits   (Page 50)
            Fade to spot on Curly

SCENE 16. Night

To open: As Scene 1

Cue 8   **Jenny** exits   (Page 53)
            Fade to spot on Curly

Cue 9   **Curly:** "Back to my guns"   (Page 53)
            Fade to Black-Out

EFFECTS PLOT

PART I

SCENE 1

Cue 1   As Scene opens   (Page 1)
            Announcer and music—"String of Pearls"—on speaker

Cue 2   **Jenny:** ". . . her fair share."   (Page 3)
            Music ends, clapping

Cue 3   **Curly:** "But I've quietened down."   (Page 4)
            Announcer and music—"Under a Blanket of Blue"

Cue 4   **Jenny:** ". . . seat of your chair."   (Page 5)
            Music ends, clapping

Cue 5   **Jenny:** ". . . out of the country."   (Page 5)
            *Announcer and music—"We'll Gather Lilacs"—continue over
              scene change then fade*

SCENE 2

Cue 6   **Mrs Dunning:** "Good night."   (Page 12)
            *Music—"For All We Know"—continue over scene change
              then fade*

SCENE 3

Cue 7   **Curly:** ". . . poor bloody wogs."   (Page 13)
            *Music—"For All We Know"—continue over scene change
              then fade*

SCENE 4

Cue 8 **Curly:** ". . . lump of gristle." (Page 16)
Music—continue over scene change then fade

SCENE 5

Cue 9 **Patrick:** ". . . off my table." (Page 21)
Music—"We'll Gather Lilacs"—continue over scene change then fade

SCENE 6

Cue 10 **Curly:** ". . . know what she felt." (Page 23)
Music—"Blanket of Blue"

Cue 11 **Curly:** ". . . racket to be in." (Page 24)
Music off

Cue 12 **Curly** exits (Page 25)
Music—"Blanket of Blue"—continue through scene change then fade

SCENE 7

Cue 13 **Patrick:** "Put your clothes on." (Page 26)
Music—continue until end of scene

SCENE 8

Cue 14 Before scene begins (Page 26)
Sound of sea, continue through scene

Cue 15 After Jenny exits (Page 29)
Sound of car starting up and departing

Cue 16 **Curly:** ". . . bomb into submission." (Page 30)
Music—"We'll Gather Lilacs"—full orchestral version

PART II

SCENE 9

Cue 17 **Jenny:** ". . . the most highly educated." (Page 31)
Music—fade a single cello. Continue through scene change

SCENE 10

No cues

SCENE 11

Cue 18   **Jenny:** ". . . men's ever-darkening lives."   (Page 36)
            Music—continue through scene change then fade

SCENE 12

Cue 19   **Curly** exits   (Page 40)
            Music—"We'll Gather Lilacs" (played Lomax-style)—continue through scene change and until Cue 20

SCENE 13

Cue 20   **Curly:** "Just shut up."   (Page 40)
            Music falters to a stop

Cue 21   **Lomax:** "Let's Bossa Nova."   (Page 41)
            Music—"Bossa Nova"—continue through scene change then fade

SCENE 14

Cue 22   **Curly:** "I was in."   (Page 44)
            Music—continue through scene change then fade

SCENE 15

Cue 23   **Curly:** ". . . Shadow of the Moon."   (Page 50)
            Music—"We'll Gather Lilacs"—very loud volume. Continue through scene change then fade

SCENE 16

No cues